# The Truth About Dogs

# THE TRUTH ABOUT DOGS

## Volker Kriegel

Translated and introduced by
## Julian Barnes

WHISKY SMELLS LIKE DOG SMELLS LIKE WHISKY SMELLS LIKE DOG SMELLS LIKE WHISKY SMELLS

**BLOOMSBURY**

First published in Great Britain 1988
This paperback edition published 2005

Originally published under the title
*Kriegels Kleine Hunde-Kunde* by Haffmans Verlag

Copyright © 1986 by Haffmans Verlag AG Zürich
Introduction and translation © 1988 by Julian Barnes

Guest Dog on page 1 drawn by Tatjana Hauptmann

The moral right of the author has been asserted

Bloomsbury Publishing Plc, 36 Soho Square, London W1D 3QY

A CIP catalogue record for this book is available
from the British Library

ISBN 0 7475 7852 4
9780747578529

10 9 8 7 6 5 4 3 2 1

Printed in Great Britain by Clays Ltd, St Ives plc

All papers used by Bloomsbury Publishing are natural, recyclable
products made from wood grown in well-managed forests.
The manufacturing processes conform to the environmental
regulations of the country of origin

www.bloomsbury.com

For Ev
but also for Juli, Nico, Joles
and all the others

# Introduction

The trenchant and beguiling masterpiece you are about to enjoy has three shameful British prejudices to overcome. The first is our sturdy belief that the Germans, while objects of ripe mirth in themselves, are incapable of being funny. The second is our shockingly tolerant notion that a collection of badly drawn cartoons can be just as amusing as a book of well-drawn ones. And the third is our incomprehensible addiction to books about cats.

The British have always asserted that the German sense of humour is about as real as the Swiss Navy (though personally I've always assumed that the prudent Swiss kept a small flotilla tucked away somewhere in the Mediterranean, just in case). This fairly harmless contention can be comforting, even necessary – look, they may have all the Deutschmarks and most of the BMWs but we're the ones with the sense of humour; yet it's getting harder and harder to defend. For many years my own prejudice was just as reliable as the next person's, despite growing evidence that the Germans had in fact figured out how to laugh. At first we admitted that, oh, sure, they knew about being *satirical* (Grosz, Brecht/Weill and all that). Irony? Yes, they might have mastered that. OK, they could be scurrilous. Mocking? Yup. Gently droll? Well, perhaps so (didn't *Heimat* surprise us?). Ah, but could they be *funny*? This zig-zagging tactical retreat went on for a long time and depended, of course, on the constant redefinition of *funny* in terms of what the Germans were *not*.

I finally surrendered this increasingly hopeless position

7

last year in the departure lounge of Hamburg airport. It was six o'clock on a gloomy evening incorrectly billed as Spring. It had rained all day; I had seen nothing of Hamburg except through the spattered window of a car; I had read my work to a gathering of forty in an auditorium better suited to one of Hitler's medium-sized rallies; I had failed to sell a single copy of any of my books; and I had been paid just about enough to cover my duty-free. Now I was sitting with a clanking plastic bag among cheery Eurobusinessmen who knew much better than me how to vend their wares, and gazing out of the window at the low cloud, the steady rain, the skiddy runway. Idly, and without expectation, I picked up *Kriegels Kleine Hunde-Kunde* which someone had thrust on me after my reading. Within five pages I was restored to good humour; within ten I was snorting with laughter and a stranger to embarrassment; within twenty I was putting the book away for fear that Lufthansa would turn me back at the departure gate on the ground that I'd taken a dangerous dose of stimulants.

So I had. However, I had discovered not just a very funny cartoonist but also a draughtsman of rich variation and cunning line. Two of the more dismaying recent trends in Humour have been the rise of the cartoonist who can't draw and the tyranny of the caption. The first indicates a crazy democratization of the profession – everyone has a few cartoons inside them, along with the inevitable, unpublishable novel; the second is a nefarious vogue which can perhaps be traced back to the *New Yorker*. The cartoons in that magazine are extremely funny, but too often represent the triumph of the caption-writer (or a caption-rewriter like Peter de Vries). The draughtsman's contribution may be no more than de-lineating the frown of a husband and the glare of a wife, or vice versa: the drawings are merely there to set you up for the captions. In Volker Kriegel's work, the captions set you up for the drawings, and the drawings make you laugh. This seems to me the right way round.

So we are now in the presence of a genuinely funny German cartoonist who draws beautifully. The final problem is: he's chosen to depict dogs. This might not seem a difficulty, given that the British are famous dog-owners, dog-lovers, dog-shampooers, dog-buriers, and so on. But it is. In this country there are approximately six million dogs and six million cats; yet this equality of love and purchase is quite forgotten as soon as a member of our nation goes into a bookshop. When Mr Desmond Morris produced two companion volumes called *Dogwatching* and *Catwatching*, he found that the latter outsold the former in a ratio of two to one. *Catwatching* was even discovered selling well at dog shows. Why should this be? Are cat-owners more literate? Do they all live in city flats with potted plants and buy the latest paperbacks, whereas dog-owners live down muddy lanes miles from the nearest bookshop? Is there some connection between curling up with a cat and curling up with a book? Is dog-exercising a thorough psychological substitute for reading? Do cats like the quiet rustle of a turning page and dogs prefer the more vigorous stimulation of television? Do dogs bully their owners into not reading? Do dogs eat books? These are all matters requiring serious study.

This book tells you the truth about dogs, truth which is tender as well as sardonic. Dogs, for all their considerable faults, are what they are, and do not pretend otherwise; it is their owners who are devious, unpredictable, embarrassed and sentimental. The human race is distinctly fortunate that dogs have not yet learned how to blush. Volker Kriegel's little book is steeped in canine knowledge and drawn with the full growl of infuriated affection. It goes without saying that Herr Kriegel is himself a dog-owner; indeed, three-quarters of the dedicatees of this work have four legs and a tail. I suggest that *The Truth About Dogs* be put on sale at all cat shows.

*Julian Barnes*

12   Dogs are noisy

**14**   Dogs shit everywhere

16    Dogs have fleas

18    Dogs like to throw up on the carpet

20   Dogs are gluttons

Dogs behave like the worst male chauvinist   21

Dogs have bad breath

Dogs are impudent    23

Dogs fart

26   Dogs are dim

Dogs have no pride 27

28 Dogs are indiscreet

30  Dogs are demonstrative

32    **Dogs stink**

**34**    Dogs are silly

**36** Dogs are playful

Dogs ask for trouble     39

# A Comparison of Breeds I

# A Comparison of Breeds II

## The Natural Enemies of the Dog

a)

b)

c)

. . . not forgetting:

d) The Jogger

Dogs are unfair

54    Dogs can be bribed

Dogs hide their smelly bones all over the place

58    Dogs have little ear for music

Dogs ruin every holiday

. . . after year

**66    Dogs really love to eat socks**

# A Comparison of Breeds III

'The fascinating thing about him is his directness, his spontaneity, his – how can I put it? – his unruliness, that whiff of anarchy, that . . . forgive me, my dear . . . that proletarian aroma.'

'Sure, he's as stubborn as an old goat – does precisely as he pleases – loves rolling in shit – loses his hair like mad – you keep finding it on the sofa and the pillows – my trousers and coat are covered in it – and of course he's filthy, well, they all are – and he drools like an imbecile, and it's incredible the way he's always got slobber hanging out of his gob – plus which he gets me out of bed at half five every morning – *and* he's just taken up snoring – but, you know, in spite of it all, believe it or not, he's got . . . something – yes, when all's said and done, he's really got . . . something'

'Relax. It's just he can smell you're afraid of him.'  75

AND SOMETIMES
HE HAS THIS REALLY
FUNNY LOOK

LIKE WHAT ?

'It's the ideological side of things that really gets me. The fact is, the psychopathology of dogs is riddled with crypto-Fascist elements. It's revolting how easily they get fixated on some Führer figure. And then there's the whole business of precedence, hierarchy, authority, obedience – it's all extremely sinister. Of course they do need a firm hand. You don't get anywhere with anti-authoritarian sweet-talking. Only a couple of days ago, I was *forced* to punish him, right in the middle of the street, for getting into a fight with another dog. I'd only given him the slightest of taps on the rump with a copy of the *Guardian* when a couple of cretins started accusing me of being an authoritarian pig and cruelty to animals. Someone even called me a sadist. This damn dog is making me play a role I really hate. I can't take it any more.'

84　Dogs like to pee behind the sofa

There are dogs which are quite happy, long after their first
youth has fled, to play the fool in exchange for a mere inch    85
of spaghetti

86   Dogs are jealous

PRINCE!

HERE, PRINCE!

3)

# PRINCE !!
# COME
# HERE
# THIS
# INSTANT !

4)

# GET A
# MOVE ON

89

5)

6)

AND WHAT CAN
THE LITTLE
DOGGIE DO ?

7)

CLEVER BOY,
PRINCE

Towards the close of the twentieth century
dogs increasingly took over those positions and functions
traditionally allotted to children

The Dog and the Car.

That's another story . . .

Dogs are flash

. . . not to mention
**The Dog and the Motorbike**

Dogs are expensive

**108** Adolf H. ('The Führer') with his alsatian ('Prince')

Frederick II ('The Great') with his greyhound ('Serge')     109

110     Arthur S. ('Schopi') with his poodle ('Atma' aka 'Butz')

Elizabeth II ('The Queen') with two of her
corgis ('Myth' and 'Fable')

Dogs have to be walked every single day

. . . and in absolutely every weather

Dogs can get very old